Macmillan/McGraw-Hill TIME

The United States

Student Practice and Activity Workbook

 Macmillan/McGraw-Hill
Glencoe

The McGraw·Hill Companies

 Macmillan
McGraw-Hill

Send all inquiries to:
Macmillan/McGraw-Hill
8787 Orion Place
Columbus, OH 43240-4027

ISBN: 978-0-02-151741-1
MHID: 0-02-151741-X

Printed in the United States of America.

8 9 10 MAL 15 14 13

© McGraw-Hill

Grade 5 Workbook
Table of Contents

Unit 5

Unit 6

Unit 7

Unit 8

Meet the First Americans

For each statement below, use one of the groups in the box to identify the speaker.

hunter-gatherer	Olmec	Ancestral Pueblo
Hohokam	Maya	Mississippian

1. Workers in my civilization built stone pyramids and temples to honor our gods. _____

2. I crossed the Beringia Land Bridge when I followed the animals I hunted. _____

3. In the kiva in our cliff dwelling, we held meetings and religious ceremonies. _____

4. I lived in the great city of Cahokia, one of the largest cities in the world. _____

5. My people were the first to eat *cacao* beans, and the first American people to use a zero in our calculations. _____

6. We built canals to carry water to our fields, where we grew maize and other plants. _____

Write Your Own

Write a sentence that a person in one of these groups might say. Then ask a classmate to figure out the speaker's group.

_____

_____ Speaker: _____

CURRICULUM CONNECTION   MATH

Comparing Time Lines

Read the information on both time lines, then answer the questions.

The Hohokam

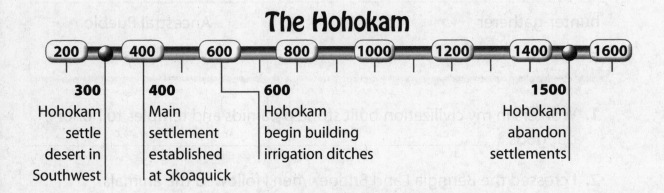

300
Hohokam
settle
desert in
Southwest

400
Main
settlement
established
at Skoaquick

600
Hohokam
begin building
irrigation ditches

1500
Hohokam
abandon
settlements

The Ancestral Pueblo

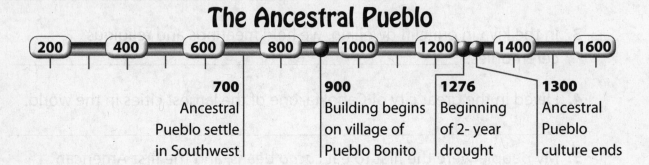

700
Ancestral
Pueblo settle
in Southwest

900
Building begins
on village of
Pueblo Bonito

1276
Beginning
of 2- year
drought

1300
Ancestral
Pueblo
culture ends

1. What is the time span shown on each time line?

_____

2. Which group settled in the Southwest first? When?

_____

3. Based on the two time lines, could the Ancestral Pueblo have learned
   about irrigation ditches from the Hohokam? Explain your answer.

_____

Life in the West

Fill in this chart with information about Native Americans of the West.

	Arctic	California Desert	Pacific Northwest
Groups	Inuit		
Climate			
Food sources			

Pueblo or Navajo?

Circle the correct group for each statement.

1. They live in a dry land that receives only a few inches of rain each year.

   Pueblo   **Navajo**   **both**

2. Their name also describes their adobe homes, which look like apartment buildings.

   Pueblo   **Navajo**   **both**

3. They farm with a method called dry farming that irrigates with tiny dams and canals.

   Pueblo   **Navajo**   **both**

4. Their ancestors migrated to the Southwest from Alaska and Canada.

   Pueblo   **Navajo**   **both**

5. Diné is another name for this people.

   Pueblo   **Navajo**   **both**

6. The Hopi and Zuni people are part of their group.

   Pueblo   **Navajo**   **both**

7. Their dome-shaped homes are called hogans.

   Pueblo   **Navajo**   **both**

Living on the Plains

Answer the questions using complete sentences.

1. How did horses change life for the Plains peoples?

_____

_____

2. What things did bison provide for the Plains peoples?

_____

_____

3. How are earth lodges made differently from teepees?

_____

_____

4. In what ways did the Plains peoples use fire?

_____

_____

5. What useful skills did girls and boys on the Great Plains learn?

_____

_____

_____

CURRICULUM CONNECTION **LANGUAGE ARTS**

A Call for Action

Imagine that you are Hiawatha or Deganawida. Write a speech to convince the warring Iroquois people that they should live in peace and create the Iroquois Confederacy. Use the space below to take notes, then write your speech on a separate piece of paper.

In your speech you should include:

- strong reasons why the Iroquois groups need to work together.

- ideas about how to create a confederacy.

Present your speech to the class. Ask for feedback. Which of your arguments was the most convincing?

© McGraw-Hill

Vocabulary Review

Choose a word from the box for each definition.

glacier	clan	civilizations
migrate	travois	archaeologists
potlatch	wampum	irrigation

1. People who study tools, bones, and remains of ancient people

_____

2. Supplying dry land with water through pipes and ditches

_____

3. A feast celebrated by Native Americans of the Pacific Northwest

_____

4. To move from one place to another _____

5. A thick sheet of slow-moving ice _____

6. Populations that share systems of trade, art, religion, and science

_____

7. A kind of sled that is dragged to move supplies _____

8. A valuable string or belt of seashell beads _____

9. A related group of families _____

Discovering Other Cultures

As Europeans began to explore the world, they discovered ideas, people, and places that were new to them. Circle the correct word or words that complete each sentence below.

1. Around the year A.D. 1000, Vikings were the first Europeans to reach:

Denmark   **North America**   **Africa**

2. Crusaders hoped to capture Jerusalem from the:

Vikings   **Europeans**   **Muslim Turks**

3. Marco Polo and his family saw many new things when they lived in:

Jerusalem   **Greenland**   **China**

4. Prince Henry of Portugal started a school to teach:

trade   **navigation**   **religion**

5. By sailing around the tip of Africa, Bartolomeu Dias reached:

Europe   **Portugal**   **the Indian Ocean**

6. Vasco da Gama sailed from Portugal to:

Jerusalem   **India**   **Denmark**

Think About It What effect did trade have on the religion that West Africans followed? Write your answer on a separate sheet of paper.

Name _____   Date _____

Mapping Locations

Understanding latitude and longitude helps you find places on a map. Follow the directions to label this map, then answer the questions.

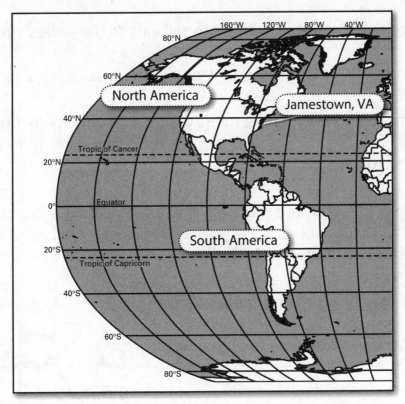

1. Trace one line of latitude on the map. Label it **LA**

2. Trace one line of longitude on the map. Label it **LO**

3. What is the nearest absolute location of Jamestown?

_____

_____

4. What is the relative location of North America from South America?

_____

_____

Columbus Arrives

Read each statement. Write **True** or **False** after the statement.
If false, write the reasons for your answer on a separate sheet of paper.

1. Christopher Columbus wanted to sail east to the Indies, the same

direction that Vasco da Gama went. _____

2. Columbus approached the rulers of Portugal and Spain, but no one

wanted to pay for his voyage. _____

3. The ships of Columbus reached North America, but Columbus believed

that they had landed in the Indies. _____

4. When they first met, the Taíno and the

Spaniards were friendly towards each

other. _____

5. The Columbian Exchange was

the money that Spaniards paid

to the Taíno for the land

they took. _____

© McGraw-Hill

Comparing and Contrasting Empires

Though the Aztec and Inca empires had certain things in common, they also were very different. Use the numbered descriptions below to complete the Venn diagram that compares and contrasts the two empires. Write the numbers in the correct parts of the diagram. The first one has been done for you.

Aztec Empire   Both   Inca Empire

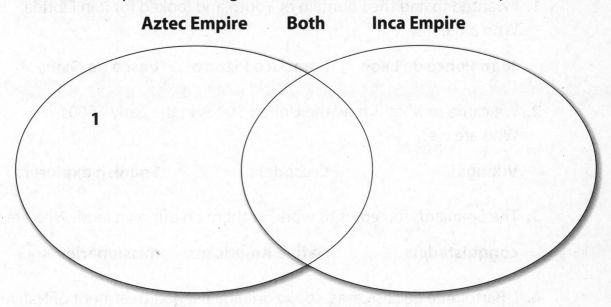

1. Located in present day Mexico

2. Cuzco was its capital

3. Tenochtitlán was its capital

4. Conquered by Hernan Cortés

5. Moctezuma II was its ruler

6. Spaniards looked for gold there

7. Atahualpa was one of its rulers

8. Located in present day Peru

9. Many people there died of smallpox

10. Conquered by Francisco Pizarro

11. Spaniards brought horses there

12. Mexico City was built on the ruins of its capital

13. Was the wealthiest empire in the world

14. Used quipus to remember information

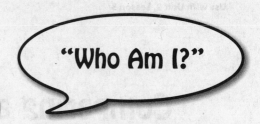

Who's Who in New Spain

As the Spanish empire in North America grew, it changed the lives of Europeans, Africans, and Native Americans. Circle the name of the correct person, group, or term described in each riddle below.

1. I wanted to find the Fountain of Youth and looked for it in Florida. Who am I?

Juan Ponce de Leon   **Francisco Pizarro**   **Vasco da Gama**

2. We came to what is now the United States in the early 1500s. Who are we?

Vikings   **Crusaders**   **Spanish explorers**

3. The Spaniards forced us to work for them on our own land. Who are we?

conquistadors   **Native Americans**   **missionaries**

4. I, Bartolome de Las Casas, spoke out against bad treatment of Native Americans. What do I do for a living?

merchant   **missionary**   **conquistador**

5. In 1570, I led a rebellion with 800 followers. Who am I?

Cabeza de Vaca   **Yanga**   **Bartolome de Las Casas**

6. I was the leader of New Spain. Who am I?

a missionary   **a Viking**   **the viceroy**

Name _____ Date _____

Use Two Graphs

Graphs can tell you about history in different ways. Use Graphs A and B to answer the questions below about the slave trade.

Graph A

Where Enslaved Africans Were Taken, 1500-1870

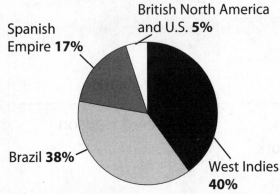

Spanish Empire **17%**

British North America and U.S. **5%**

Brazil **38%**

West Indies **40%**

Graph B

Enslaved Africans Brought to the Spanish Empire, 1500-1870

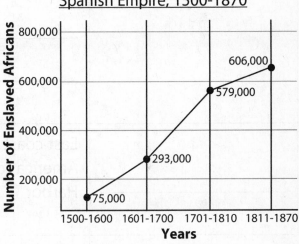

75,000

293,000

579,000

606,000

Number of Enslaved Africans

800,000

600,000

400,000

200,000

1500-1600 1601-1700 1701-1810 1811-1870

Years

Source: Oxford Atlas of World History

1. According to Graph A, where were the largest numbers of enslaved

   Africans taken? _____

2. According to Graph B, about how many total enslaved Africans were

   taken to the Spanish Empire between 1500 and 1870? _____

3. According to Graph B, did the arrival of enslaved Africans to the Spanish

   Empire increase or decrease over time? _____

Charting Explorers

Fill in the name of the correct explorer and places to complete this chart.

Explorer	Area Explored	Results
John Cabot	_____ _____	Discovered rich fishing grounds
_____	East coast of North America to New York Harbor	Discovered Hudson River
Henry Hudson 1st voyage	_____ _____	Discovered Hudson River was not the Northwest Passage; believed area around river would be good for settlement
Henry Hudson 2nd voyage	_____ _____	Did not find the Northwest Passage; there was a mutiny on his ship

Name _____   Date _____

Settling New France

Fill in the blanks with the correct word or words to complete the sentences below.

1. In 1534 Jacques Cartier claimed a peninsula near the St. Lawrence River

for the country of _____.

2. The explorer _____ founded a fur trading post at Quebec.

3. Native Americans from the Algonquin and _____ groups

became allies of the French.

4. _____ was the first French explorer to see Lake Huron.

5. _____ was the first European to see Lake Superior.

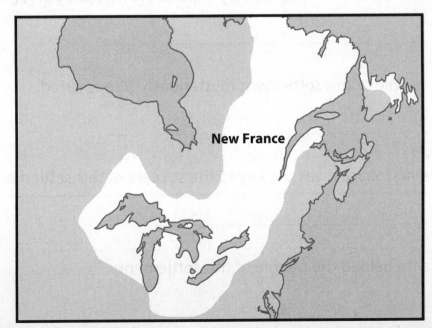

Name _____   Date _____

What Happened Where?

Roanoke, Jamestown, and Plymouth were early English efforts to settle North America. After each description below, write the name of the correct settlement being described.

Roanoke   **Jamestown**   **Plymouth**

1. The Virginia Company sent 105 men and boys to begin this settlement:

   _____

2. Captain John Smith played a major role in the survival of this

   settlement: _____

3. Sir Walter Raleigh sent two expeditions out in an attempt to settle

   this colony: _____

4. This settlement was founded by Separatists who set out for Virginia:

   _____

5. The people of this settlement mysteriously disappeared:

   _____

6. Growing tobacco was the key to the success of this settlement:

   _____

7. Squanto helped the people of this settlement: _____

Vocabulary Review

Write the letter of each term next to its correct meaning.

a. profit	**d.** missionary	**g.** charter
b. expedition	**e.** mestizo	**h.** cash crop
c. colony	**f.** export	**i.** indentured servant

1. ___ money that remains after the costs of running a business

2. ___ someone who worked for another in exchange for food, shelter, or travel

3. ___ someone who teaches religion to those with different beliefs

4. ___ to send goods to another country for sale or use

5. ___ an official document that grants it holder special rights

6. ___ a region controlled by a distant country

7. ___ a person of both Spanish and Native American heritage

8. ___ a crop that is grown to be sold for profit

9. ___ a journey with a special purpose

Famous New England Names

Who might say each of the things below? Write the correct name from the speech bubble.

Anne Hutchinson   Roger Williams

John Winthrop   Metacomet

1. Our "city on a hill" will show people how God wants them to live.

_____

2. Governments should tolerate different religious views.

_____

3. Colonists should not take any more land. _____

4. People can understand the Bible on their own.

_____

Think About It What is something Thomas Hooker might say?

_____

_____

_____

A Trip through the Middle Colonies

Suppose you could go back in time and visit the Middle Colonies. Who might you meet there? In the chart below, write each person or group from the box under the correct colonies. Watch out: you might find some groups in both places!

William Penn	a Swedish colonist	a Scots-Irish colonist
an enslaved African	a Quaker	a Mennonite
a proprietor		

New York and New Jersey	**Pennsylvania and Delaware**

Think About It Who are some other people you think you might meet in the Middle Colonies? Add your ideas to the chart.

Which Southern Colony?

Circle the correct colony below each description.

1. Where wealthy colonists built large rice plantations

North Carolina   **South Carolina**   **Maryland**

2. Settled by debtors

Georgia   **Virginia**   **South Carolina**

3. The Toleration Act was passed here

Carolina   **Georgia**   **Maryland**

4. Split into two colonies in 1729

Maryland   **Carolina**   **Georgia**

5. Became a trade center because of Charles Town's excellent harbor

Maryland   **Carolina**   **Georgia**

6. Its silk industry failed

Carolina   **Maryland**   **Georgia**

Rice

Living in the Colonies

What kind of work might these people have done in colonial times?
Write a brief description next to each of the people listed below.

1. indentured servant _____

_____

2. woman _____

_____

3. apprentice _____

_____

4. backcountry settler _____

_____

Cause and Effect

Use the graphic organizer below to write one cause and one effect of
the Yamasee War.

Cause:

_____

_____

_____

→ **The Yamasee War** →

Effect:

_____

_____

_____

Settling the Colonies

Learn more about English settlement of the thirteen colonies. Use the map on page 123 of your textbook to help you answer these questions.

1. What is the symbol for a colonial capital? _____

2. Which capital is farthest south? Which one is farthest north?

_____

3. What nation claimed territory west of the Appalachian Mountains?

_____

4. Was more land settled in Georgia or Virginia by 1760?

_____

5. Before 1660, were most settlements along the coast or inland?

_____

6. Why do you think much of the land settled between 1700 and 1760 was farther inland rather than on the coast?

_____

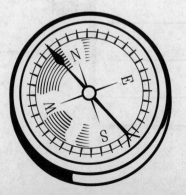

Enslaved Workers

Use a complete sentence to answer each question below.

1. What was the Atlantic slave trade? _____

_____

2. How did the slave laws change over time? What caused this change?

_____

_____

3. Did Northern farms or Southern farms use more enslaved workers? Why?

_____

_____

4. What is one reason enslaved Africans told traditional stories?

_____

_____

5. What are two ways enslaved Africans resisted slavery?

_____

_____

The Triangular Trade

Fill in the blanks to complete this diagram of the Triangular Trade.

Traders sailed from New England

to (**1**)_____ with such

goods as rum, iron, and

(**2**) _____. They traded

the goods for (**3**) _____.

On what was called the Middle

Passage, traders took captives

from (**4**) _____

to (**5**) _____.

There the Africans were sold

into (**6**) _____.

In the Caribbean, ship captains

bought (**7**) _____ and

molasses to take back to

(**8**) _____. There,

the molasses was made into

(**9**)_____.

© McGraw-Hill

True or False?

After each statement, write **T** if it is **True**.
If it is **False**, rewrite the sentence so it is correct.

1. Colonial assemblies were responsible for making laws that were good for England.

_____

2. Everyone could vote in the colonies.

_____

3. Colonial governors had greater loyalty to the king or proprietor than to the colonists.

_____

4. At New England town meetings, colonists discussed local problems.

_____

5. John Locke wrote about people's natural rights to life, freedom, and property.

_____

6. Peter Zenger went on trial for writing poems about enslaved Africans' natural rights.

_____

Vocabulary Review

Which word belongs in each sentence? Write the letter of the correct word or phrase in each blank.

a. tolerate	**d.** debtors	**g.** industry
b. patroons	**e.** Great Awakening	**h.** assembly
c. plantation	**f.** spirituals	

1. Shipbuilding was an important _____ in New England.

2. Jonathan Edwards was one of the preachers who led the _____.

3. Roger Williams believed that government should _____ different religious views.

4. On a Southern _____ , cash crops such as tobacco and rice were grown.

5. Some of the first settlers of Georgia were _____ .

6. Most colonies had a lawmaking body called an _____ .

7. Enslaved Africans sang _____ , which are still part of American music.

8. To attract settlers to New Netherland, the Dutch West India Company offered land grants to wealthy _____ .

The French in Louisiana

Choose the correct name to fill in each blank below.

Pierre Le Moyne, Sieur D'Iberville	Robert de La Salle
Jacques Marquette	Louis Jolliet
King Louis XIV	
Jean-Baptiste Le Moyne, Sieur de Bienville	

1. The first French colonists to explore the enormous Mississippi were

   _____, a fur trader, and _____, a missionary.

2. _____ claimed the Mississippi River for France.

3. _____ decided to strengthen French control of

   Louisiana in order to prevent losing it to England or Spain.

4. _____ was the first governor of Louisiana.

5. His brother, _____, founded the city of New Orleans in 1718.

Think About It If you could meet one of the people mentioned above, what is one question you would ask him? Write your question here. What do you think his answer would be?

_____

_____

Name _____   Date _____

CURRICULUM CONNECTION ▸ MATH

Tracking the War

Create a time line of the French and Indian War. Write the letter of each event below under the correct date on the time line. Watch out! There are more years shown than events.

a) The French surrender Quebec to the British.

b) George Washington attacks French soldiers near Fort Duquesne.

c) British forces capture Fort Duquesne.

d) The Treaty of Paris is signed.

e) General Edward Braddock's army is defeated at Fort Duquesne.

| 1754 | 1755 | 1756 | 1757 | 1758 | 1759 | 1760 | 1761 | 1762 | 1763 |

____ ____ ____ ____ ____ ____ ____ ____ ____ ____

Think About It) The French and Indian War has been called "the war that made America." Why do you think it's called this? Write your answer on a separate sheet of paper.

No More Taxes!

Complete this Action–Reaction chart by filling in the blank boxes.

Action   Reaction

Action	Reaction
The French and Indian War leads to war debts for the British government.	1._____
British Parliament passes the Townshend Acts.	2._____
Colonists gather at the Boston Customs House in 1770.	3._____
Massachusetts Governor Hutchinson orders three English ships to remain in Boston Harbor in 1773.	4._____
Parliament passes the Intolerable Acts.	5._____

Name _____ Date _____

Who Did What?

Read the clues and fill in the blanks to determine who did what, and what impact their actions had. For number 3, choose another historical figure from Lesson 4 and create your own chart.

1.

| **Who:** Paul Revere | **What he did:** Rode to warn colonists of British soldiers approaching Lexington, Massachusetts |

Impact of his actions: _____

2.

| **Who:** _____ | **What he did:** Led the Green Mountain Boys, a militia unit from Vermont |

Impact: _____

3.

| **Who:** _____ | **What he did:** _____ |

Impact: _____

Declaring Independence

Decide whether each statement below is true or false. Write **T** or **F** after the statement. If a statement is **false**, circle the letter right next to it. Then, unscramble the circled letters to spell the name of a member of the committee appointed to write the Declaration of Independence.

1. When the Second Continental Congress met in May 1775, all of the delegates were in agreement. _____ **H**

2. King George agreed to repeal the Intolerable Acts after reading the "Olive Branch Petition." _____ **A**

3. After the king's response to the petition, the delegates decided to try talking to him again. _____ **E**

4. One reason why the Congress chose George Washington as commander of the army was his southern background. _____ **L**

5. Congress believed that the colonies could pay for the war on their own. _____ **R**

6. Congress began writing the Declaration of Independence on July 4, 1776. _____ **N**

7. Thomas Jefferson's first draft included an attack on slavery. _____ **P**

8. The Declaration said that the colonists would consider remaining as British subjects if the king acted differently. _____ **S**

9. All of the delegates signed the Declaration of Independence on July 4, 1776. _____ **M**

Hidden Name: _____

Army Versus Army

Identify the strengths and weaknesses of the British and American armies by circling the correct name under each description.

1. Was a large, well-organized army of 60,000 soldiers

British Army   **American Army**

2. Was aided by Loyalists

British Army   **American Army**

3. Soldiers signed up for six months

British Army   **American Army**

4. Supplies were shipped across a long distance

British Army   **American Army**

5. Could attack by surprise

British Army   **American Army**

Think About It Study the strengths and weaknesses charts on pages 172 and 173 in your textbook. Suppose you lived in the colonies at the beginning of the American Revolution. Based on what you know about the two armies, who would you have predicted to win the war? Why? Write your answer on a separate sheet of paper.

Name _____   Date _____

Following a Battle

The Americans suffered some early defeats at the beginning of the Revolutionary War. Use the map on this page to answer the following questions.

The Battle of Long Island, August 1776

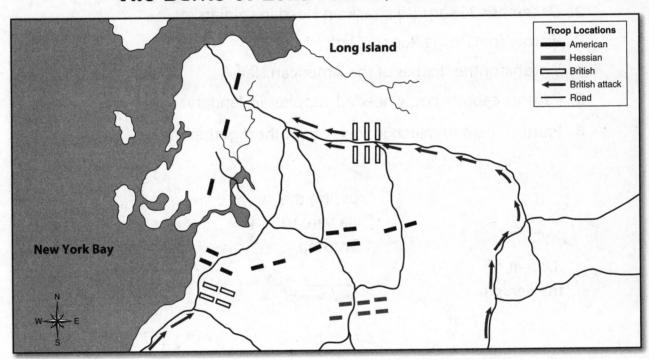

1. What is the subject of this map? _____

2. What armies fought in this battle? _____

3. In the map key, circle the symbol that stands for the British attack. On the map, use a colored pencil or marker to trace the routes of the British attack.

4. From what two directions did the British attack the Americans?

_____

Patriot Successes

Each numbered item below describes a Patriot success in the years between 1776 and 1779. Place the number of each event in the correct circle.

1. Turning point of the Revolution

2. December 25 surprise attack on Hessian soldiers

3. Victory for George Rogers Clark

4. Victory for the "Father of the American Navy"

5. Patriots capture badly needed supplies in January

6. Patriots learn to march in rows and fight together

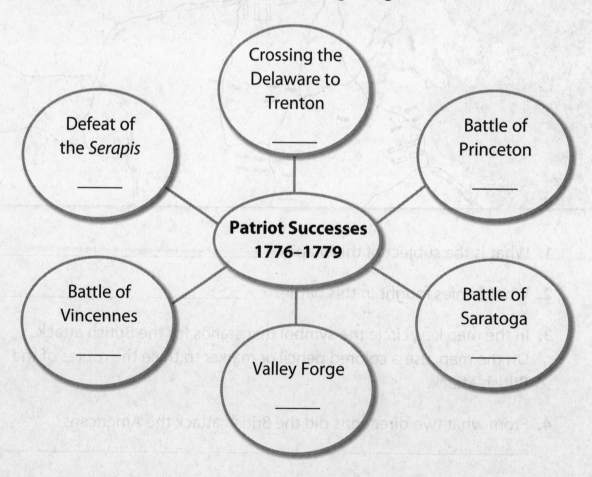

Name _____   Date _____

The Americans Win!

Track the last days of the Revolution by filling in the blanks in the flowchart below.

1. General _____ takes command of the British army in the South in 1780.

→

Cornwallis and his men track the Americans through the Carolinas.

↓

3. In the summer of 1781, Cornwallis leads _____ men to _____, Virginia.

←

2. In March of _____, the two armies finally meet at _____.

↓

This proves costly to Cornwallis and the British.

→

4. _____ is a spy for Marquis de Lafayette.

↓

This traps Cornwallis and his men, and they are not able to receive supplies.

←

5. Lafayette alerts the _____ navy, who set up a _____ of British ships.

↓

George Washington and a large French army join the attack, forcing Cornwallis to plan an escape.

→

6. However, the escape is stopped by_____. Cornwallis finally surrenders on _____.

Vocabulary Review

Use the clues to fill in the crossword puzzle with vocabulary words.

Across

1. a stream that leads into a larger river

2. to run away from military service

Down

3. making profits off of goods that are in short supply

4. to refuse to buy goods or services from a person, group, or country

5. a colonist who supported Great Britain

Lie Detector

Can you find the truth about early United States history? Read each statement below. If it is true, write **T** after the statement. If it is false, write **F** and then rewrite the sentence on a separate piece of paper to make it true.

1. The first United States government needed money to pay lawmakers and soldiers who had served in the Revolution. _____

2. The Northwest Ordinance created a plan for settling land north of the Great Lakes and west of the Snake River. _____

3. Shays's Rebellion showed that the Articles of Confederation worked well. _____

4. Under the New Jersey Plan, the legislature would have one house, in which each state would have one vote. _____

5. The Great Compromise created the Articles of Confederation and the Electoral College. _____

6. Under the Three-Fifths Compromise, every five enslaved people counted as three free people. _____

7. Benjamin Franklin is known as the "Father of the Constitution." _____

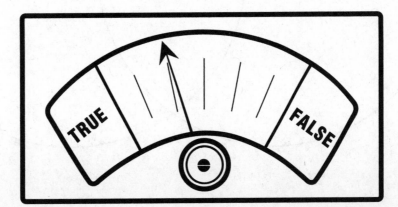

Two Ways to Govern

Compare the Articles of Confederation with the Constitution. Write the letter of each item below in the correct part of the Venn diagram.

a. Plan of government for the 13 states

b. Gave the national government the power to pass taxes

c. States had their own money and trade laws

d. Included a Congress

e. Created in 1777

f. National and state governments shared power

g. Led to Shays's Rebellion

h. Used the system of checks and balances

i. Established a legislature with two houses

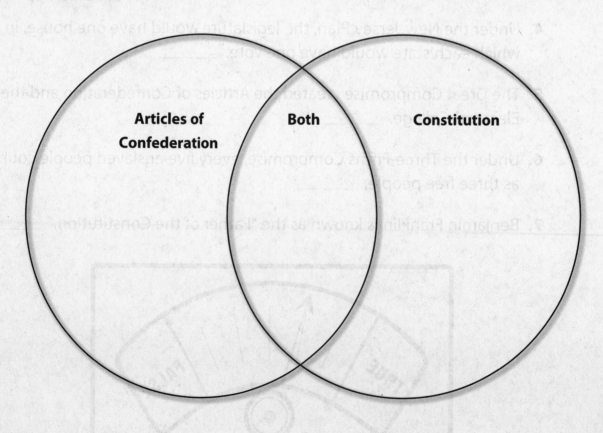

Articles of Confederation   **Both**   **Constitution**

Double or Nothing

Suppose you were the President of the United States, and you had the opportunity to double the size of the nation's land area today. Would you do it? What would be the advantages and disadvantages for the U.S. and for the people who lived in the newly added territory?

On a separate sheet of paper, write a speech explaining your decision. In your speech, discuss the nation's rapid growth through the Louisiana Purchase. How did this influence your decision today?

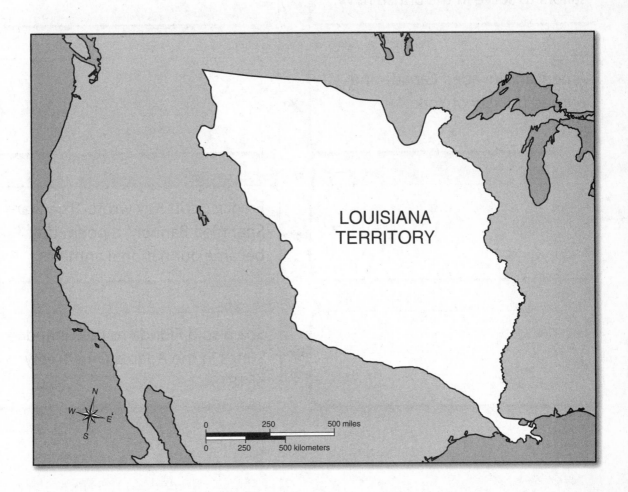

LOUISIANA TERRITORY

Fighting for Control

Complete the Cause and Effect chart by filling in the empty boxes.

Causes: ## Effects:

The British aided Native Americans in the West and forced American sailors to serve in the British navy.	→	

Americans invaded Canada and burned the city of York.	→	

	→	Francis Scott Key wrote "The Star-Spangled Banner," a poem that became our national anthem.

	→	Spain sold Florida to the United States in the Adams-Onís Treaty of 1819.

Different Maps, Different Scales

Use the two maps on page 221 in your textbook to answer the questions below.

1. Which map would you use to determine troop location during a battle? _____

2. Which map shows state borders? _____

3. Which map has a larger map scale? _____

Think About It

4. Why do the two maps have such different map scales?

_____

_____

5. What kind of research can you do with Map A? Map B?

_____

_____

Big Changes

Write the name of the correct invention or development after each description. Then write its number in the correct circle in the web below.

1. Pieces made to fit any specific product _____

2. Machine with sharp blades to cut grain _____

3. A man-made waterway connecting Lake Erie to the Hudson River and

Atlantic Ocean _____

4. Robert Fulton's invention _____

5. The "iron horse" _____

6. A factory where workers turn cotton into cloth _____

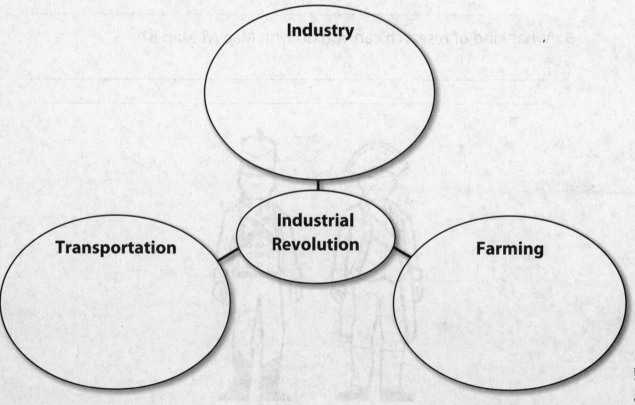

© McGraw-Hill

Name _____ Date _____

The Jackson Era

Circle the correct answer for each question.

1. How did the office of President change under Jackson's leadership?

became more powerful   **became less powerful**   **did not change**

2. Why did South Carolina leaders threaten to leave the Union?

a new Constitution   **to let women vote**   **new tax**

3. Where did the Indian Removal Act force Native Americans to go?

Arizona   **Indian Territory**   **Texas**

4. What belief encouraged Americans to move west?

Indian Removal Act   **Manifest Destiny**   **the Union**

5. Which group settled what is now Salt Lake City?

Cherokee   **Mormons**   **Native Americans**

6. Problems with what crop led many Irish people to come to America?

corn   **bison**   **potatoes**

7. By 1840, what was happening to the nation's population?

decreasing   **increasing**   **staying the same**

A Growing Nation

Place the historical events of Texas and California in order. Number the events from 1 to 10.

_____ Gold is discovered near Sacramento.

_____ The Mexican government offers land to Americans in Texas.

_____ Texas becomes an independent country.

_____ The United States declares war against Mexico.

_____ California becomes the 31st U.S. state.

_____ Thousands rush to California to find gold.

_____ The new Texans complain about Mexican laws and want to legalize slavery.

_____ Stephen Austin and an army of Texans attack San Antonio.

_____ General Sam Houston defeats Mexicans at San Jacinto.

_____ Mexico and the United States sign the Treaty of Guadalupe Hidalgo.

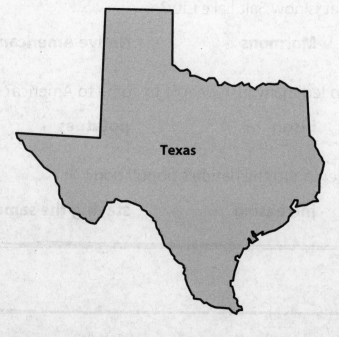

Texas

California

Vocabulary Review

Read each pair of words or phrases below. Choose the word from the box that best fits each pair. Write the word on the line.

| legislature | union | amendment |
| ratify | discrimination | |

1. approve   accept   _____

2. change   addition   _____

3. lawmakers   branch of government   _____

4. group   joined together   _____

5. prejudice   unfair treatment   _____

Write **C** next to the phrases or names below that are related to the Constitution.

_____ interchangeable parts   _____ Manifest Destiny

_____ federal system   _____ legislature

_____ impressment   _____ Supreme Court

_____ Bill of Rights

Cotton at the Center

Complete this cause and effect chart.

Cause	Effect
Cotton weakened the soil where it was grown.	1. So, planters moved _____ to find new land.
Raising cotton as a cash crop required a large work force.	2. Therefore, the demand for _____ grew.
3. _____ wished to enter the Union as a slave state in 1819.	4. In order not to upset the balance of slave and free states, the _____ admitted one free and one slave state.
British factories could manufacture goods more cheaply than Americans could.	5. British manufacturers could sell goods to Americans at a _____ price.
Americans who owned small factories could not compete with the British.	6. Congress passed _____ on British goods.

Use with Unit 6, Chart and Graph Skills

Study a Climograph

Use the climograph on page 249 in your textbook to answer the questions.

1. What does the line graph show? _____

2. What does the bar graph show? _____

3. What are the two wettest months in Memphis? _____

4. What is the coldest month? What are the average high and low temperatures in this month? _____

_____

5. Using the climograph, how would you describe summers in Memphis?

_____

_____

_____

Before the Civil War

Choose the correct name to complete each sentence below.
You will not use all the names.

William Lloyd Garrison	Abraham Lincoln
Frederick Douglass	Angelina Grimke
John Brown	Stephen Douglas
Harriet Beecher Stowe	

1. The *North Star* was published by _____,
   an abolitionist who had escaped from slavery.

2. With her novel *Uncle Tom's Cabin*, _____
   turned many Americans against slavery.

3. _____ introduced the Kansas-Nebraska
   Act in the Senate, proposing that voters could decide whether to accept
   or ban slavery.

4. The election of _____ as President triggered
   the secession of Southern states.

Place these events in the correct order, from **1** to **5**.

_____ Civil War begins   _____ John Brown's raid

_____ Lincoln-Douglas debates   _____ Abraham Lincoln elected
                                          President
_____ South Carolina secedes

A Nation at War

Place the number of each description in the correct part of the Venn diagram below. Then add your own ideas.

1. Had a strong military tradition

2. Had a largely untrained army

3. Had more factories and railroads

4. Had better skill in shooting, hunting, and riding

5. Thought the war would last about two months

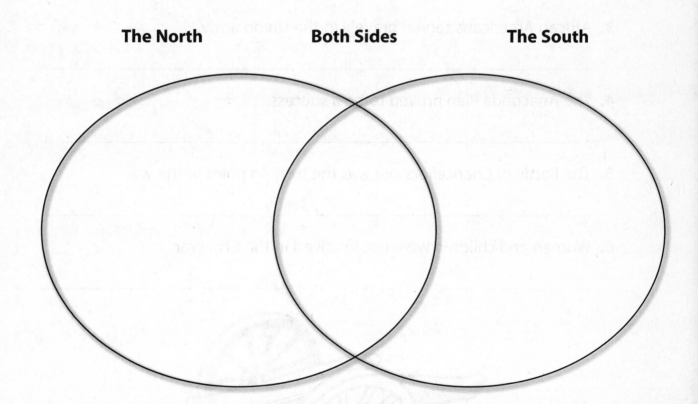

The North   **Both Sides**   **The South**

Name _____   Date _____

Toward Victory

Read each statement. Write **True** or **False** after the statement. If the statement is false, write the reasons for your answer.

1. The South won the battle at Antietam in an easy victory.

_____

2. The Emancipation Proclamation declared that all enslaved people were free.

_____

3. African Americans served bravely in the Union army.

_____

4. The Anaconda Plan proved to be a success.

_____

5. The Battle of Chancellorsville was the turning point of the war.

_____

6. Women and children were not involved in the Civil War.

_____

© McGraw-Hill

The End of the War

Answer the questions about the end of the Civil War.

1. In the final battles of the war, which general was in charge of the entire Union Army?

   _____

2. Which important railroad center did Union forces put under siege for ten months?

   _____

3. Which general terrorized the South in order to break its fighting spirit?

   _____

4. The fall of what city helped Lincoln win reelection?

   _____

5. Where did General Lee surrender to General Grant?

   _____

Write a Poem On a separate sheet of paper, write a poem expressing the country's sadness about the assassination of President Lincoln. You can use the quotation from Walt Whitman on page 279 of your textbook for ideas.

Name _____   Date _____

Reconstructing the Nation

Complete the chart to show what the government did to rebuild the nation.

Government Action	What It Accomplished
Freedmen's Bureau	1. _____ _____
Reconstruction Act of 1867	2. _____ _____
Thirteenth Amendment	3. _____ _____

 **Think About It**

4. Why was Andrew Johnson so unpopular?

_____

_____

5. What did *Plessy v. Ferguson* uphold as constitutional?

_____

_____

Vocabulary Review

Answer the questions below by circling the correct term.
First try to complete the activity *without* looking in your textbook.

1. As an _____ , Frederick Douglass spoke out against slavery.

   abolitionist   **adventurer**

2. Southerners threatened to _____ from the Union if Lincoln were elected.

   move   **secede**

3. John Brown was convicted of _____ against the United States.

   trickery   **treason**

4. John Wilkes Booth was guilty of the _____ of Abraham Lincoln.

   assassination   **election**

5. Jim Crow laws made _____ in the South legal.

   segregation   **education**

6. What plan involved surrounding the Confederacy?

   the Sherman Plan   **the Anaconda Plan**

7. In which address did Lincoln describe the purposes of the Civil War?

   the Second Inaugural Address   **the Gettysburg Address**

8. Which government order ended slavery in Confederate states?

   the Emancipation Proclamation   **the Proclamation of 1763**

Settlers Move West

Circle the correct word or phrase to complete each sentence.

1. On cattle drives, cowboys guided cattle from ranches in _____ to railroads in Kansas.

   Illinois   **Texas**   **California**

2. The discovery of _____ in California increased the need for a transcontinental railroad.

   gold   **oil**   **cattle**

3. The Pacific Railway Act granted _____ to companies to build the railroad.

   workers   **land**   **cattle**

4. It took _____ years to complete the transcontinental railroad.

   five   **six**   **seven**

5. Homesteaders claimed land on the _____.

   Sierra Nevadas   **Great Plains**   **transcontinental railroad**

6. The Homestead Act said a head of a household could claim _____ acres of land.

   160   **150**   **180**

© McGraw-Hill

Conflict on the Plains

In the boxes on the left are two main ideas from Lesson 2. Fill in important details about each main idea in the boxes on the right.

Main Ideas	**Details**
1. As settlers and railroads moved in, many Native Americans lost their way of life.	
2. Conflicts over land led to clashes between U.S. soldiers and Native Americans.	

CURRICULUM CONNECTION SCIENCE

Inventions that Changed America

Answer these questions about inventions of the late 1800s.

1. What are three important inventions made by Thomas Edison in the late 1800s? _____

2. Who invented the telephone? _____

3. Who worked as an assistant to both Edison and Bell? _____

Think About It Sometimes new technologies replace earlier ways of doing things. For example, over time some people started listening to the phonograph instead of playing musical instruments. What might other inventions from the late 1800s have replaced?

- The electric light replaced _____ .

- The telephone replaced _____ .

- Moving pictures replaced _____ .

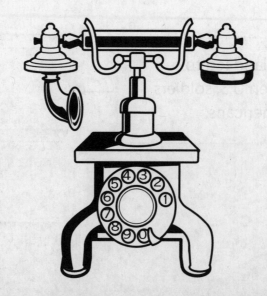

Name _____ Date _____

The Truth about Growing Cities

Decide whether each statement below is True or False. Write **T** or **F** after the statement. If it is false, explain the reasons for your answer.

1. In the 1860s most Americans lived in large cities. _____

_____

2. Many cities grew up around a single industry. _____

_____

3. A majority of immigrants that came to America between 1870 and 1924 came from Northern and Western Europe. _____

_____

4. Most immigrants found an easy life in America. _____

_____

5. Jane Addams worked to make immigrants' lives better. _____

Think About It Suppose you worked in a settlement house in the late 1800s or early 1900s. What are some ways you could work to help immigrants? Write your answer on a separate sheet of paper.

Name _____   Date _____

World Population

Use this cartogram to answer the questions below.

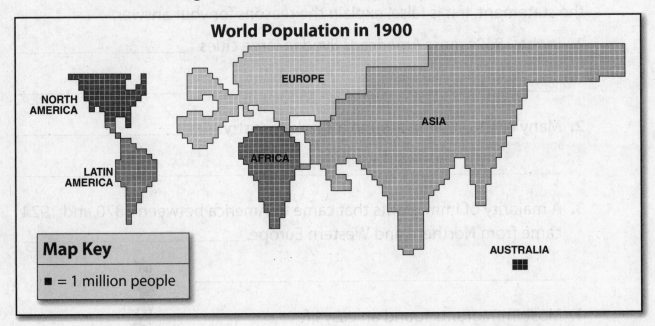

World Population in 1900

EUROPE

NORTH
AMERICA

ASIA

AFRICA

LATIN
AMERICA

AUSTRALIA

Map Key

■ = 1 million people

1. What does the cartogram show? _____

2. What does each square stand for on the cartogram? _____

3. According to the cartogram, which continent had the largest population
   in 1900? _____

4. Which continent shown had the smallest population? _____

5. Look at a world map in an atlas. Is Europe larger or smaller than Africa on
   a world map? On the cartogram? What does this tell you? _____
   _____
   _____

Alaska, Hawaii, and More

Write the letter of each description in the correct section on the chart. You will need to use one letter twice.

a. Captain Cook landed there in 1778

b. Sold to the U.S. in 1867

c. 1959

d. Annexed by the U.S. in 1898

e. Owned by Russia

	ALASKA	HAWAII
Early European Contact		
U.S. Takeover		
Became a State		

Complete each sentence.

1. The sinking of the *Maine* led to the _____ .

2. After the war, the U.S. gained the territories of_____

_____ .

Vocabulary Review

Draw a line from each word to the correct definition.

1. homesteader

2. property rights

3. reservation

4. monopoly

5. cattle drive

6. slum

7. annex

8. Buffalo Soldiers

a. person who claimed 160 acres under the Homestead Act

b. a business that completely controls an industry

c. a rundown neighborhood

d. the rights to own or use something for sale

e. territory set aside for Native Americans

f. a journey where cowboys guided cattle from ranches to railroads

g. to take over an area of land

h. African American soldiers who had fought in the West

Use with Unit 8, Lesson 1

Causes and Effects in the Early 1900s

Fill in the empty boxes to complete this cause and effect chart about the early 1900s.

Causes

Effects

> There was a wide gap between the rich and poor.

1. _____
_____
_____
_____

> American businesses wanted a better way to ship products between the Atlantic and Pacific Oceans.

2. _____
_____
_____
_____

> Archduke Francis Ferdinand of Austria-Hungary was assassinated.

3. _____
_____
_____
_____

> 4. _____
_____
_____
_____

> The United States entered World War I.

Use with Unit 8, Map and Globe Skills

What Time Is It?

Use the time zone map on page 331 in your textbook to answer the questions below.

1. How many time zones are there in the United States? _____

2. When it is 9 A.M. in New York, what time is it in Chicago? _____

3. When it is 11 A.M. in Denver, what time is it in Jacksonville? _____

4. When it is 2 P.M. in Seattle, what time is it in Dallas? _____

5. What time zone do you live in? _____

6. Suppose a friend from Honolulu wants to call you when you get home from school at 4 P.M. What time in Honolulu would your friend have to call? _____

Think About It Why do you think some time zone lines follow national or state borders instead of perfectly straight lines? Write your answer on a separate sheet of paper.

© McGraw-Hill

Changing Times

Circle the correct word or phrase to complete each sentence.

1. For about 100 years American women had been fighting for suffrage, or the right to _____.

   war   **vote**   **jobs**

2. _____ laws took away African Americans' right to vote.

   Suffrage   **Jim Crow**   **Amendment**

3. The movement of African Americans from South to North is called the _____.

   Great Awakening   **Great Depression**   **Great Migration**

4. The assembly line process was developed by _____.

   Jim Crow   **Henry Ford**   **Herbert Hoover**

5. Larger audiences for media such as magazines, movies, and radio led to a growth in _____.

   advertising   **assemblies**   **allowances**

6. The National Origins Act limited _____ to the United States.

   innovation   **immigration**   **emigration**

7. President Roosevelt proposed the _____ as a way to end the Great Depression.

   New Deal   **Square Deal**   **New Deed**

Fighting World War II

The bolded word in every sentence about World War II is **false**. Replace this word with a term that makes the sentence **true**. Write your answer on the line.

1. Germany, Italy, and Japan were known as the **Allied** Powers. _____

2. Dictator Adolf Hitler was the absolute ruler of **Italy**. _____

3. Hitler attacked the Soviet Union in **1945**. _____

4. The United States declared war on **France** after the attack on Pearl Harbor. _____

5. **Hundreds** of American women went to work during the war. _____

6. The armed forces were **integrated** during the war. _____

7. D-Day was the beginning of an enormous invasion of **the Soviet Union**.

_____

Think About It Suppose you are an American soldier who has been serving in Europe or the Pacific during World War II. You just got news that the war is over. On a separate sheet of paper, write a letter home expressing your feelings about the American victory.

© McGraw-Hill

A Different Kind of War

Answer these questions with complete sentences.

1. Why was the conflict between the U.S. and the U.S.S.R. called a "cold war"?

_____

_____

2. Who first used the term "Iron Curtain," and what did it mean?

_____

_____

3. What was the arms race?

_____

_____

4. How did President Kennedy respond to the Cuban missile crisis?

_____

_____

Think About It Suppose you lived in the United States during the 1950s. What would be some of your fears and hopes for the country's future? List your ideas in the boxes below.

Fears:

_____

_____

_____

_____

Hopes:

_____

_____

_____

_____

Big Changes

Write the correct name or phrase from the boxes to fit each description.

| Brown v. Board of Education | Rosa Parks |
| The Great Society | Martin Luther King, Jr. |

1. This court case declared that separate but equal facilities were unconstitutional. _____

2. Segregation on public buses was declared illegal partly as a result of this person refusing to change seats on a bus. _____

3. This civil rights leader made a historic speech during the March on Washington. _____

4. President Johnson called his dream for America by this name.

_____

Draw a line to match each group with its actions.

Organization	Actions
1. UFW	a. demanded fairness and respect for Native American treaties
2. NAACP	b. fought for better conditions for migrant workers
3. NOW	c. fought against segregation
4. AIM	d. protested for equal rights for women

Moving Forward

Write these events in the order they occurred on the lines below.

- U.S. invasion of Iraq

- Persian Gulf War began

- U.S. invasion of Afghanistan

- formation of Al Qaeda

- bombing of the World Trade Center

- attacks on the World Trade Center and the Pentagon

1. _____

2. _____

3. _____

4. _____

5. _____

6. _____

Complete this chart by filling in details for each main idea statement.

Main Idea	Details
Countries around the world are increasingly interdependent.	
The growth of the global economy has led to environmental problems.	

Vocabulary Review

Each definition below describes the *opposite* of one word in the box.
Write the word and its *correct* definition next to each opposite definition.
An example is done for you.

| prejudice | reform | global warming | assembly line |
| truce | suffrage | neutral | internment |

1. *Example:* A process in which a product is built by one person <u>assembly line: a process in which a product is built as it moves past workers</u>

2. A change to make people's lives worse _____

_____

3. Denying people the right to vote _____

_____

4. Decrease in the average temperatures on Earth _____

_____

5. Taking sides _____

_____

6. Integrating people during a war _____

_____

7. An agreement to begin a war _____

_____

8. A negative opinion based on experience and proof _____

_____